THE ABC Kids BOOK OF

Places to Go

For the children who keep us young — HM & JS
For Benedict and Jakob — CO

First published in Australia in 2017
Paperback edition published in 2018
by HarperCollins*Children'sBooks*
a division of HarperCollins*Publishers* Australia Pty Limited
ABN 36 009 913 517
harpercollins.com.au

HarperCollins*Publishers*
Level 19, 201 Elizabeth Street, Sydney NSW 2000, Australia
Unit D1, 63 Apollo Drive, Rosedale, Auckland 0632, New Zealand
A 53, Sector 57, Noida, UP, India
1 London Bridge Street, London SE1 9GF, United Kingdom
2 Bloor Street East, 20th floor, Toronto, Ontario M4W 1A8, Canada
195 Broadway, New York NY 10007, USA

A catalogue record for this book is available from the National Library of Australia

ISBN: 978 0 7333 3428 3 (hardback)
ISBN: 978 0 7333 3429 0 (paperback)

Cover illustrations by Cheryl Orsini
Designed and typeset by Megan Bond
Colour reproduction by Graphic Print Group, Adelaide
Printed and bound in China by RR Donnelley on 128gsm Matt Art

7 6 5 24 25

THE ABC Kids BOOK OF

Places to Go

HELEN MARTIN JUDITH SIMPSON CHERYL ORSINI

So many different places —
special things to do —
— places like the garden,
the shops and library too.

All kinds of different places —
some you know but some are new!

A place to play outside …

Do you have favourite things
to do in the garden?

koo-koo-koo-koo-koo-koo-kaa-kaa-kaa!

There are

Scissors snip — click, clack —
cutting hair front and back!

Up and down between the shops,
the escalator never stops.

many different places to visit at the shopping centre.

Hooray! Hooray!
New shoes today!
Stepping out to walk and play!

The library is a quiet place to borrow books.

Choose a book.

Listen to a story.

Time for a check-up at the medical centre.

Everyone waits in turn to see a doctor or a nurse.

Measure — how tall?
Weigh — how heavy?
Breathe in!
Breathe out!
Say a-a-h!
SWITCH OFF

Places close to home, places far away …
Sail by boat
Ride a horse
BINDY WINDY STATION
LIBRARY
Take a train
Drive in a car

Fly by plane
BINDY CAVES
ZOO
CAKES
TAXI
TAXI
Catch a bus
Take a taxi
Ride a bike
Walk
How would you travel?

At the noisy airport planes fly off to faraway places.

Queue up to check in
for safe boarding.

Where could you go today?
EXIT

Some places keep collections of things.

Inside a special room at the museum
there are very old dinosaur bones.

Outside at the butterfly farm
beautiful butterflies flutter in the sunshine.

The zoo is a place where many animals live. Zookeepers take care of them.

What animals can you see?

Different places … different things to do …

Slide in a snowy place.

Ride in a country place.

Glide in an icy place.

Hide in a
secret place.

Going up! There are tall buildings above the ground.

Climb to the lighthouse.

Step up,
up,
up.

The light helps ships sail safely round the rocks at night.

Going down! There are large limestone caves below the ground.

Where can you see these things?

Laugh, kookaburras!

Fly up and away
to a new place today …

Stripy tiger, awesome growl,
hungry creature on the prowl!

Flutter by, butterflies …

A warning light at night …

Dancing, hopping,
starting, stopping!

A place to play inside …

Where is your favourite place?

So many different places —
— special things to do —
— places like the doctor's,
museum, lighthouse, zoo.

All kinds of different places —
some you know but some are new!

Explore the world with the ABC Kids BOOK OF series!

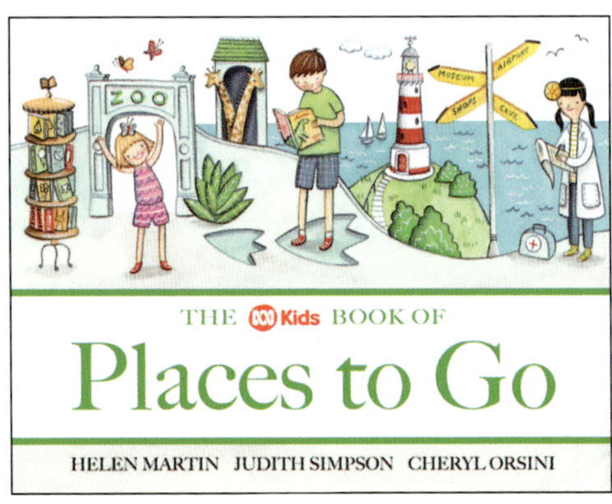